Clouded Thoughts

Michael Froilan

Copyright © 2021 by Michael Froilan Chavez Bugay

All rights reserved. No part of this publication may be reproduced or transmitted in any form or by any means, electronic or mechanical, including photocopying, recording, or any other information storage and retrieval system, without the written permission of the publisher.

COVER ILLUSTRATION: Sabina Kencana

ISBN: 9798701656633

I am writing this not for the eyes of the many,

but for yours alone:

for each of us is audience enough for the others.

- Epicurus

ACKNOWLEDGEMENTS

Ma and Pops, without the two of you, this book wouldn't have life. Thank you for gifting me my independence. Because of you, I am resilient. I am courageous. I am determined. Your love is better than life itself. I will live with unending gratitude to have been raised by both of you.

Francis and Mark, I wouldn't be as fearless and unyielding if it weren't for our brotherhood and how competitive we were growing up. Thank you for illuminating honor and loyalty.

Laura, thank you for enriching my life with your love, acceptance, understanding, encouragement and support. You inspired me to take a chance on this book. Your light is an undeniable presence. Thank you for never shying away from showing how much you care.

Oreste, thank you for pushing my drive and adaptation. Here's that mixtape you've been waiting for.

To all my family and friends, you are all a blessing in disguise. Each of you has enlightened me more than you know. Thank you.

I love all of you.

CONTENTS

- CLOUDED THOUGHTS 11
- 6 AM TRAIN RIDES 12
- DERAILED 13
- MOVEMENT 14
- ROUND AND ROUND 15
- CONFLICTION 16
- SLOW DEATH 17
- BARBED ACCEPTANCE 18
- SELF-RIVALRY 19
- REAWAKENING 20
- SNUBNOSED 22
- CAST 23
- PAY DIRT 24
- G-WAY 25
- WITHOUT A CLUE 26
- MIRROR YOU 27
- THREE WORDS 28
- INDOCTRINATION 29
- WHAT'S WHAT 30
- INTERSECTIONS 31
- UPPER HAND 32
- CONCRETE ISLAND 33
- AVERAGING DOWN 34
- SPARK 35
- SPINE 36
- ESSENCE 37
- STUPEFY 38
- NEW DAY RESOLUTIONS 39
- SADNESS TO HEART 40
- EARTH DAY 41
- UNFOLD 42

PIGMENTATION	43
STAY UP	44
MOONWALKER	45
DISBARRED	46
CLOAKS	47
SWEET VIRGO GIRL	48
SET APART	50
GODSEND	51
MONUMENTS	52
Q AND A	53
WHATLESS	54
DEAR ENEMIES,	55
PRICE TAGS & EXPENSES	56
WHY I WRITE	57
ELEMENTARY	58
ECLIPSE	60
MR. ROGERS 2020	61
FOREIGN UNDERSTANDING	62
BEGET	64
SPROUT	65
UNMATCHED	66
BARRIERS	67
BASEBALL BAT ON THE WALL	68
STUNNING CALAMITY	70
DELICACY	71
CARRY ON	72
COGNITION	73
OVERLAY	74
QUIETUDE	75
LOST AND FOUND	76
CONTAINER	77
CEMENTED REMINDER	78
EVERYDAY THANKSGIVING	79
GANDER	80

JIGSAW	81
NOCTAMBULIST	82
MONEY OR TIME	83
SYMMETRY	84
SCUFF	85
RIDGES	86
NOTHING LASTS	87
PULSE	88
TRIED AND TRUE	90
AWAKE	91
I KNOW HER	92
SOVEREIGNTY	93
BROUGHT LOW	94
CATCH DRIFT	95
OBVIOUSLY	96
$U¢¢E$$	97
FISHEYE	98
SKIN DEEP	99
2 OF CUPS	100
CALL TO MIND	101
FILTERED EXISTENCE	102

CLOUDED THOUGHTS

My feet planted on hell,
My thoughts above the heavens.
On the road less travelled
It always feels like I hit a dead-end.
But I make way and keep to stepping,
It's nothing new to me.
You see,
Truthfully,
There are no obstacles,
There are only opportunities.

6 AM TRAIN RIDES

The crummy seats are taken up by
strangers with familiar work schedules.
Restlessness painted on everyone's expressions.
Bags under the eyes like it's a stylish trend.
Faces as long as the day ahead.
Flashes of forced smiles and defensive scowls.
The conversations are empty like most people's brains.
Makes sense, I guess.

Words go one ear and out the other like cotton swabs.
How did I forget my headphones?
Anyway, silence comforts me
no matter how awkward it is to some.

The train screeches
mirroring the sound of misery of having to work a 9 to 5.
I choose to start two hours early.
It's my way of finding
the loophole to a dose of happiness.

Not only is this cart polluted with distress,
dreams and ambitions sift through the air.
Racism is half asleep during commutes (so I think).

It doesn't seem to matter
the colour of our skin.
Oddly enough,
we are all judged by the collar of our jobs.
So much for being different.

DERAILED

It's rush hour.
The rubber-legged cars are sprinting
towards an unknown finish line.

I watch them dash by and catch a glance
of each driver's sullen look.
Smiles buried six feet deep within their hearts.
Red lights don't halt their misery.
Burning rubber to earn money to burn.

What a competition it is.
This human race
has gone so far
but not gone anywhere.

Take reality and drive it home.

Roads have been paved,
yet plenty of people are more off-track than trains are.

MOVEMENT

Rock bottom is a dead-end,
Nothing takes place there.
The only upside is it's safe.

Like everyone else
I've reached this fixed point before
And carelessly enjoyed comfort in the gloom.
I settled for a while
Until I realized
Time waits for nobody.

No matter how long
You forget the world,
It doesn't care about your feelings,
Your thoughts, your deeds.

Acknowledge this now,
Recollect your virtues
And sidestep the cold ground of the wasteland.
Anchor your focus at the infinite skies
That seem to dance away in harmony.

Time to make things happen.
Nothing always leads to something.
All it takes is action.

ROUND AND ROUND

Trees tango with the wind.
Clouds sailing across the horizon.
The sun is going on its way.
The day shift has punched out.
It's time for the moon to take over.

Funny how darkness exposes
Most people's fears.
Why is it that
When you try
To shed light on secrets,
The more they hide?

Leave them in the dark
And they don't shy away
From unveiling their undertone.

We live in a twisted world.

CONFLICTION

Crickets serenade the silence of the empty streets.
One moment my eyes are open as my consciousness.
And next, they are folded shut like my heart.

My thought patterns are out of shape.
Good luck figuring out
the geometry of my mind.

It's a constant battle between
lifting my spirit
and breaking down these demons.

SLOW DEATH

Some of us live hoping
we can leave behind
a legacy worth remembering.
And when we doubt our abilities,
we kill ourselves slowly.

BARBED ACCEPTANCE

We are a lot like roses.
Each of us has thorns planted in our flesh
Signifying our imperfections.

Many allow their flaws
To pick and tear them apart.
While just a few pick up on
How to humbly embrace
The beauty deeply rooted in themselves.
And by doing so,
This is how they gracefully bloom.

SELF-RIVALRY

There's a tug of war
between love and hate
taking place in my heart.
The real struggle is trying
to stand firm on the side I'm on.

Am I like everyone else?
Divided and warring with myself
rather than finding and making peace?

Sometimes for your own good,
it's just best to push your pride aside,
draw in and pull out the white flag.

REAWAKENING

Today I find myself
looking in the mirror,
searching for answers.

An aspect of me is about to die.
Maybe I know which it is,
Maybe I don't.
I don't sweat it.
Every moment something is changing.

Regeneration is routine.
We are not the same person overnight.
Some would argue that we are.
I say it's our outlook that doesn't switch on impulse.

Today's sunrise won't be the same hereafter.
We can't spot the wind alter
but it's happening
before our aging eyes.

As far as one can tell,
change is encouraged
until your betterment makes others unsettled.

Your improvement will cause discomfort.
You will soon encounter
those who think they know you
striving to remind you of your past
rather than exerting energy to facilitate their future.
The worst of you is what they'll use
to try to disfigure your refinement

- A sad case of crab mentality.

There's a difference between change and transformation.
A lot get old but never mature.

Millions will go to bed tonight and sleep on themselves.
Tomorrow they will wake up and smell the coffee, but they won't rise.

Some want to level up.
Some only want leverage over others.

SNUBNOSED

Most individuals live with their hearts disguised.
They avoid being the nail that sticks out,
scared stiff of getting hammered by opinions.
Forgetting the fact that
opinions are hardly ever knowledge.

It's natural to have insecurities,
but mentally choking yourself out by them is not.
Only the gutless are overdressed in pretention.
To be fearful of being yourself is the worst attire there is.

Your confidence must be tough as nails.
Don't be rattled by judgment.
As hard as they try to strike you down,
they won't be able to dismantle your spirit.

Choose not to die with a mask on.

CAST

Shed;
You possess all
The tools you need
Within you.

Discard your hardened armour.
Despite the crossfires you go through
In the battlefield of life,
Your soul will remain intact
When the smoke clears.

Trust that.

Shed and dispose of
Your foolish vanity.

PAY DIRT

No matter how successively we win,
We must take our fair share of losses
In order to strike gold.
You're never really defeated,
Unless you willfully give up.

It's a disadvantage being pessimistic.
I mean, it's normal to feel weak sometimes,
But to choose to stay weak is straying from yourself.

Don't waste away.
After all,
We don't know Strength until we meet Weakness.

G-WAY

My neighbour approached my friend and I mid-conversation.
He asked for a cigarette,
Homeboy handed him a cancer stick
And he fired away.

Inhale and out comes a narrative
About some local pusher he looks up to.
Project tales of making dough
And having strippers occupy the passenger seat.
This broadcast was airing in an empty church parking lot.

I glanced up at the stars gleaming
Behind the icy darkness of the winter night sky.
Zoning out as the broken record kept playing,
I reflected about the dullness of the spirit.
I thought about Neighbourhood Watch.

Over the years, I witnessed my neighbour transition
From a curious boy
To the delirious man that stood before me.
He's a product of the projects.
He's a *blockhead*.
Not stupid I hope,
But his mind is evidently filled with hood dreams.
Dreams generated by misguidance and ignorance.
Aspirations constructed by falsehood.
It's comical and saddening
How differently we humans define
Success and happiness.

WITHOUT A CLUE

Her smile staggers me.
Her eyes always capture
My attention without fail.

She's an enigma
Unaware of her nature.
I'm eager to know
Everything there is about her.
She knows this.

She humbly emphasizes she's nothing special.
I strongly deny her view about herself.
I think she needs to buy a new mirror.

MIRROR YOU

Is it strange to say that I want to be your mirror?
I want you to see
that even your flaws are beautiful.
I want to show you
what your dazzling eyes are blind to.

I marvel at your existence.
Elegance isn't hard to find when you're facing me.
Your presence is a spectacle.
Sometimes I'm paralyzed by
that eye-catching smile.
Anyone is blessed to witness it.

I'm dazed,
observing the windows to your gentle soul.
I notice they conceal
the quiet strength and resilience that you downplay.
Doubt has smeared your lens.
I'll rub away the blur for you to realize your brilliance.
I won't hesitate to point out your glow.
To remind you of fire out of sight that you overlook.

Is it strange to say I want to be your mirror?

Let me prove to you how truly beautiful you are.

I seek for you
to reflect on
the woman I see in you.

THREE WORDS

Seagulls plague the plastered blue sky
Giving rise to thoughts of freedom.
I lay my eyes on the rolling water
As the sun glares unapologetically.

Ripples of reflection.
The consoling clamour of waves
Stifles the chatter of my mind.

"Prove them wrong."
My uncle pierced this phrase in my brain
Over lunch one winter afternoon.
It's been reverberating in my skull ever since.

He didn't mention who "they" were,
So, it has me thinking…

Who do I prove wrong?

My adversaries?
My family?
My friends?

Myself?

INDOCTRINATION

We as a society have been brainwashed
for so long that we become
aggressive toward those who point out
how dull we really are.

It's amusing to witness
how easily humans fall
to manipulation and
unconsciously conform.

Turn away from following suit as best you can.
And if it means traveling alone, then so be it.
Pound the pavement toward the high road.
Don't yield to become another statistic.

WHAT'S WHAT

I've learned a lot from dark times.
It has enlightened me
In so many ways.

What makes life more interesting
Is knowing
I still have a lot to learn.

INTERSECTIONS

The big hand on the clock just hit 12.
The ceiling light in my room resembles the blazing sun.
My heart is 108 km away from me.
My eyes are heavier than my emotions.
I can shut them, but my mind won't close.

There's no rest lodged in my body.
These thin walls can talk.
I haven't lost my mind yet,
Maybe my peace.

My dreams keep me up.
So do my neighbours.
I hear irritating murmurs,
Sometimes even parties of laughable stupidity.
I've always hated loud noises,
But nothing beats the dizzying silence
That rumbles in my psyche.

Ordinary people count sheep.
I often round up the minutes every other second.
The big hand on the clock is overlapping the small one.
Or is it the other way around?

The race against time.
It hasn't occurred to me until now. . .
Time runs against itself.

UPPER HAND

How often do we fail to remember
everything we have gone through?

And how empowering it is to realize
we've faced hardship
and came out victorious.

CONCRETE ISLAND

There's an island made of rubble
Where I go to press pause on life.
It's a hidden haven out in the open
Where I reflect on the fragility of existence.

I enjoy my bounded liberty a little more there,
A sanctuary where these earthly shackles weigh less.
To some, it might be bleak,
But anywhere is great
Just as long as it's far from the mundane.

Sometimes I meet up with friends there in nirvana
And we nourish our livers with cold beers.
When sobriety disappears,
Unpolished conversations swim.
That's when egos sink, and spirits rise.
I guess that's why they call it "boo"-ze.

"Old Gods in a new world."
I once read it graffitied on stone
As constant waves windsurfed
Into the body of the jagged land.

Soaking it all in at that very moment,
I have never felt so actual.
Peering through the limitless sky,
Slowly my shackles unfastened.
Take me away from the "real world".

AVERAGING DOWN

Everyone seems too caught up with economic value.
Unfortunately,
Most have lost sight of their self-worth.

SPARK

What is "perfect," really?

I look at my flaws
And turn away from Truth.
Imperfections are hard to face.

I fight off impure thoughts and focus
On the brighter side.
You see,
Even blemishes are overlooked
When placed under different lighting.

I want to shine to my brightest capacity,
But the complexion of my thoughts
Clouds the radiance of my soul.
The fire inside is dying to stay alive.
Damned if I burn out.

SPINE

To be different is to be brave.
You have to have spunk to stand out from the crowd.
The masses share similar thinking,
For the most part, at least.

Dare to be unique
And you'll find yourself
To be the center of humiliation.

They will pick you out
And try to pick you apart.

Don't let it discourage you.
Don't question your self-worth.
Never devalue yourself
Just because small minds try to belittle you.
You're better than that.
You're bigger than that.

Let them crack jokes.
Let the fools talk shit.
They can't do anything else to you.
Remember that.

Don't give power where it doesn't belong.
Especially in the hands of those who don't deserve it.

ESSENCE

This high is strange.
I've been here before.
Thoughts are sprinting without end.
No clue where to start.
All points to self.
Everybody knows that's where fate begins.

A good friend once told me to "become love".
I simply spaced-out.
How does one pull that off?

He advised not to view love
like it's a tool you obtain.
Essentially, it's what you naturally are.

You are the truth
right here,
right now.

STUPEFY

I try my best to listen as she talks,
But her beauty is enchanting.
She's expressive and vibrant.
Her modest persona oozes magnetism.
She's profoundly colourful
And sharply full of heart.
I gaze at her eyes and try to fathom
What darkness resides in her stimulating spirit.

I want to know
What her infectious smile conceals.
She's a book I'm committed to read.

I want to know her story.
I want to know
About her dreams.
Her fears.
Her weaknesses.
Her happiness.
Her rage.
Her heart.
I know I want to understand her.

Meanwhile, I try not to lose focus
As I continue to stare at this wonderful woman.
I glance away
Hoping
She spotted no sign of vulnerability.

NEW DAY RESOLUTIONS

Let it all go.
Feel your worries and fears dissipate.
Welcome in divine energy.
Protect that genuine feeling of love and joy in your heart.

Shake off your mistakes.
Nobody has it right all the time.
You can handle whatever life throws at you.
Don't be so uneasy because life is hard most times.

Don't misplace control.
Drop that feeling of putting yourself down.
Pick yourself up.
You've got mountains to move.

SADNESS TO HEART

Not everyone you meet is meant to stay in your life.
Some people are only meant to remain in your heart.
Even then and there,
Many don't belong.

EARTH DAY

I lounge on this comfy plastic chair,
thinking about the earth and why I'm here.
I glance over at the gang of trees
throwing signs and posing in front of me.

Two primary colours permeate my eyes
as the messengers of God overcrowd the skies.
The yellow burning sun endlessly beams.
The celestial sphere glows aquamarine.

My attention shifts to my heartbeat
as I silently sit and think,
How we take for granted the air we breathe
and the h2o we drink.

Now I'm reminded of my mother and father,
my dad being Air (Gemini),
my mom being Water (Pisces).
Two strong elements that gave me fire.
Grounded me,
but never deterred me from aiming higher.

They encouraged me to chase my dreams,
cautioned me about the speed bumps.
No amount of wealth will ever be
enough to repay them for helping me own my freedom.

These two gems strengthened my heart and soul.
Without their love, I'd just be another bag of bones.
I owe them the world, and that is clear.
For what is life without water and air?

UNFOLD

Grasping emotions is a tricky thing.
They always find a way to slip away.
But then again,
Maybe feelings aren't meant to be held.
And that includes the good ones too.

Excitement and expectation blind us.
We want to live beautifully
Without going through the ugly stages of life.
Yet we often forget that
The strangeness of life
Is what makes it oddly beautiful.

Progress isn't always pretty.
But eventually, you reach a level
Where every ounce of blood, sweat and tear pays off.

There's nothing more awe-inspiring than
Molding puffed up dreams
Into breathtaking realities.

All the better when you're dealing with self-growth.

PIGMENTATION

A rotten homeless man lying on the sidewalk
called me a chink while I was waiting to cross the street.
In exchange, I told him he had a lovely home.

My sarcastic compliment instantly shut him up.
He went from relentlessly cussing me out to
speechlessly flipping me off.
My girl walking next to me, said she was sorry that
happened.
I told her his remark held no weight.
It's funny because right now, I'm thinking about bigotry,
and that incident is weighing on my mind.

How can you allow yourself to get bent out of shape
about someone's skin colour?

Insecure people bring others down to keep them company
because it's the only way they can feel better about
themselves.

Racism is something I will never understand.
I'm just grateful I don't have that kind of mindset.

Don't we all bleed red?

I'm convinced that racists have infantile brains.
It would make sense.
If you're not in daycare or kindergarten,
why are you fighting over colours?

STAY UP

A lot of times,
we have no choice being around petty people.
However,
we can still choose
not to let others under our skin.

Take nothing to heart.
Otherwise,
you'll clog your being with toxic shit.
Because as you well know,
what most people say comes from their anus.

It's morbid to be narrow-minded.
It's much worse to be contaminated with negativity.

Don't buy into lower energy.
That shit is beneath you.

MOONWALKER

Give me space,
Let me ground my thoughts.
My consciousness is lost among the clouds.
Imagination travels without a destination.

Let my emotions thaw out a bit.
I've shed humanity,
Replaced it with abnormality.
I understand your confusion.

But look at this world we live in.
It's fabricated
Similar to bright smiles
Decorated on plastic faces.

Seriousness has soiled our minds.
The Gods laugh at us.
Men and women aspiring to be real
With lying truths and false personas,
Not realizing the real can't be achieved
It's something to be discovered.

This whole realm is a drama.
Scenes of light and shadows.
Pictures of duality.

I'm sorry if I'm disturbing your sleep.

DISBARRED

It's a long quiet July morning.
My wiggly thoughts are bouncing up to the cosmos.
I feel like dark coffee
steeped by the sunlight,
intoxicated by the idea of emancipation.

For years I've been slowly bending
mental bars binding my free spirit.
A prison cell put up by low self-esteem.

Sometimes I envy the egotistical
and their skyrocketing confidence,
their stuck-up arrogance.
How can one reach them
at their level of snootiness?
How can you bring them down?

Ironically,
I admire their way of freedom.

Still, I'm chipping away
with hopes to break loose
from this hell hole I dug myself in.
Only to realize

I'm holding the key.

CLOAKS

My face has more breakouts than any jail.
Lips hold a broken smile.
I stand as short as life itself.
My confidence fluctuates as the weather does.
My hopeful mind is fenced in by tedium.
My marrow is filled with bliss and suffering.
I'm leaving footprints in the sky
While remaining rooted on earth.
I'm a suspect, victim and witness of my own oppression.
It doesn't get more real than flaws,
Yet, we subtly disguise them and fake perfection.
Some are more noticeable than others.

SWEET VIRGO GIRL

I engraved your name on a wooden bench.
It seemed fitting since you're an Earth sign.
My sweet Virgo girl.
Perfect as perfect can be.

Your heart of gold is drizzling with honey,
Sweetheart.
It's no wonder why
Glucose in my blood skyrockets
Mulling over your love.

Abundance travels wherever you pass.
Where do you hide your lucent halo?
How on earth
Do you keep your wings
Tucked in your shoulder blades?

The mere thought of you induces
My heart to swell beyond the vault of heaven.
You make me feel abundant as the ocean,
And like the high seas,
My love for you is bottomless.

I'm a nomadic feathered scorpion of still waters.
You've welcomed me into your secluded island
Where shadows don't seem to exist.

I will be the downpour that drowns
Every mud-caked demon
Latching on to your inner nature.
When your life feels empty and barren,

I will nourish you tenderly
Without watering down
Your essence.

My sweet Virgo girl.
Perfect as perfect can be.
I will spoil you rotten with passion and zeal.
I will love you even when the seas go bone dry.

I am a running river.
You are a golden shore.
We are a beautiful collision.
Our hearts melting into each other.

SET APART

Silence flows
as laughter binds.
Rubber souls planted on this earth,
I'm like a wooden peg
wedged on an amputee,
why do I feel I don't belong?

It's odd
to be
singled out.
In a way,
everyone is.

GODSEND

There's buzzing energy of conceit
floating in the workplace.
I overheard this obnoxious waitress call herself an angel.
I know it's rude of me to laugh in disagreement.

Flies have wings too,
and they're full of shit.

MONUMENTS

We all got scars that tell a story.
Not only do they narrate,
They symbolize hard knocks we've endured.
They are small reminders of our strength.
Though laid out silently engraved on our skin,
They scream
For us
To keep pushing forward.

Q and A

Forgetting my expectations.
Sometimes some things don't end up
The way we mapped out.
It's no picnic wrapping awareness in the present.
Maintaining a constructive mindset is an uphill grind.

Reminding myself
To question what I worry about.
Asking why it matters
And if it should.

Life is fleeting and shifty.
Death is sure and ageless.
How meaningful is it
To be alive and encased in fear?

WHATLESS

A great deal of people can't mind their own,
because they don't have a mind of their own.

DEAR ENEMIES,

Peace be unto you.
Or pieces off of you.

Your pick.

PRICE TAGS & EXPENSES

Most things that are beautiful have an expensive price.
But everything you find unappealing also holds beauty.
You just have to pay attention.

Whatever you do,
Don't go bankrupt
Paying close attention
To the wrong things.
That list should include some people as well.

WHY I WRITE

I write because it's my meditation.
I write to remember.
I write to forget.
I write to put emotions under the knife.
I write to reach out.
I write to call out.
I write to touch base.
I write to time travel.
I write to understand life.
I write to keep my brain on its toes.
I write to let my soul speak.
I write because there are no fine lines.
I write because everything is happening all at once.
I write because I can't say one thing at a time.
I write because I hate talking.
I write because I'm an introvert with an outgoing mind.
I write to remind myself I'm deathless.
I write to remind myself I'm mortal.
I write to forgive.
I write to give thanks.
I write to analyze and observe.
I write to defeat demons.
I write to immortalize those important to me.
I write to teach the talkative how to listen.
I write to motivate the illiterate.
I write to irritate the literate.
I write to say "yes I can" to the naysayers.
I write to come to life.
I write to define love.
I write to breathe.

ELEMENTARY

I flip through a worn-out thesaurus.
This storehouse of words
has made a home on my bookshelf.
I was supposed to return it two decades ago.

Skimming through the pages,
I can't help but smirk and recollect my youth.
I remember observing my strait-laced classmates.
I recall my know-it-all neighbourhood friends.

They would attempt to lay down
the law in the playground.
I would nod and put my foot down with a grin.
They really thought I'd listen when my shoes light up?
Child, please.

Running up the metallic slide
    -   my first radical act of rebellion.
Adults said it was unsafe and impermissible.
The smart aleck kids claimed it was improper.

I was naively lawless.
Adhering only to my parents and God.
They were the only ones I let govern me.
But even then,
what child is fond of barricades?

I often overturned obstructions.
Stargazing fueled me
to surmount limitations and confinement.
Motivated to prove assumptions wrong with assertion.

I've been running up metallic slides all my life.
There's no stopping me now.

ECLIPSE

Being under your shadow
got to me sometimes
but I held admiration for you.

It's pretty foolish
to respect somebody
and resent them at the same time.

To this day, I look up to you.
Thank you for giving me the courage
to carve out my own path.

I know there will be times
my actions and decisions
won't align with your beliefs,
and you'll despise me.

Remember that I love you
and I'm not your shadow.

I have my own light to shine.

MR. ROGERS 2020

My white t-shirt soaked in sweat.
I've been reading on my balcony for fifteen minutes.
Catching some sun
before Canadian winter plagues the pending months.

Drilling noises bounce
from every direction in my area.
Tree branches wave hello.
Birds chirp and flutter through a traffic-less sky.
Time is flying along with them.
So does the ambient fragrance of Mary Jane.
I hear vehicles jogging on pavement.
Youngins posted up and scheming.
The clouds must be on vacation,
none are in sight.

A mailman wearing a surgical mask makes his rounds.
Sirens howl from afar.
Sounds like the "ambalamps".
The firetruck trails behind.

The boys in blue will catch up.
They have to make sure
the coloured man minding his business
isn't committing any crimes.

My train of thought hightails the breeze.

What a beautiful day in the neighbourhood.

FOREIGN UNDERSTANDING

I'm a yellow, black sheep.
Blending in with the crowd is not my strong suit.
I feel as though I don't belong here.
It's no matter of being in shape,
I don't fit into this world.

A wise woman once told me to cut it out.
She said I shouldn't feel like an outsider.
Maybe I'm oddly this way
Because I frustratingly can't relate
To the average person.

Sometimes I question
If I'm worthy of love.
Frequently wondering
If there's anybody in my life
Who completely understands
My independence.

Occasionally
It seems like my family doesn't accept me.
Same blood pumping in our veins,
But yet not the same at all.

I'm closed off
Even with my close friends.
I don't let anyone in.

I'm well-guarded.
But not safe from myself.

I have to remember
We all come from a place of greatness.
The only approval that matters is my own.
Learning to embrace oneness is a constant focus.

You do right by everyone when you stay true to yourself.

BEGET

Instead of thinking about what could've been,
Bring about what could be.

SPROUT

I hang on to hope
As I climb this slope.
I feel Death creeping
But Life has my back.

Love crawls all up in my thoughts.
Reality before my eyes.
I smile with confidence.

Lotuses thrive in mud
Unfazed and unscathed
By all the bullshit.

Out of challenges and suffering rises true beauty.

UNMATCHED

Her fire can burn a hole through the Sun.

BARRIERS

Do you find that you still have your guard up?
Because I want to climb over that wall
and show you that I want to be there with you.
By your side.

I want to share so much joy with you.

I want to build with you.

I want to create memories
we both can look back at and smile about.

I want to be there for you
to encourage you when you doubt yourself.

I want to assist with your growth and transformation.

I want to root you on as you chase your dreams.

I want to cheer and celebrate with you
when you achieve your goals.

I want to break down your guard
so that I can be your guard instead.
To protect you.
To be down for you
no matter what comes up.

BASEBALL BAT ON THE WALL

You bring me back to
that one day at the park
with family
where I held a green plastic bat
smiling toothless for the camera
from ear to ear.

Staring at you
brings me back
to that time
in little league,
when the batter hit a line drive
and I instinctively dove for it
thinking I was Roberto Alomar.
My jersey coated in dirt.
The feel of the softball in my clutched glove.
The crowd of parents going apeshit in the bleachers,
sounding like I performed at a sold-out Apollo.

Looking at you
reminds me of playing catch
in elementary school
during recess with my friends.
Scanning to see
where that tiny black dot
in the sky will fall and land,
scrambling to position ourselves
so we can seize the tennis ball.
Some used their bare hands.
Some wore baseball gloves.
Some even used their hats.

Staring at you
reminds me of my grandfather
who taught me the game of baseball.
Most nights before bed
I'd sit with him
and watch the Blue Jays play.
If he wasn't sipping on a beer,
he'd peel an orange and give me half.

Now my eyes are fixed at this popcorn ceiling.
Hoping my grandfather is proud of me.
Connecting the tiny white dots,
wondering
if it wasn't for baseball,
would I be a pessimist?

Because now I see,
your sight has to be forward at all times.
You have to be looking up
to catch the blessings life throws.

STUNNING CALAMITY

I fell for her like a landslide.
What she makes me feel is thundering.
Earth tremors pulsating to the core.
She is lava
tenderly burning up
my unbending heart.
My mountain of self-defence
crumbling apart.

She is a hurricane and a wildfire
madly consolidated
With might and main
Undoubtedly blowing my mind away.

DELICACY

Love is a touchy subject.
To feel it is one thing,
To scratch its surface is nearly impossible.
So many layers.
Too many forms.

Sometimes those you care about the most
Will hurt you with an iron hand.
Some would say
That's how you know it's love.
To give out a chunk of your heart
And not minding the heartaches in exchange.

Or maybe that concept is perversely wrong?
Perhaps love isn't wrapped up in pain and distress.
For all one knows,
It could be unoffending, celestial and faultless.

Love is a thin-skinned subject.
It's an entity you can't box in and pin down,
But rather something to be felt introspectively.
On the other hand,
My guess is as good as yours.

CARRY ON

Holding a grudge will hold you back.
Let go of needless baggage.
You're better off without wasted energy.
Don't let hatred taint your heart.

It's easy to stay mad,
But it's also stupid.
Don't spend another second
Obsessing over something that has already passed.
Wonderful possibilities hang right around the corner.

Clinging on to things may help with balance,
But it won't help you to move on.

COGNITION

Greatness dwells within.
There's nothing worse than slighting yourself.
Knowing the truth of your worth
is truly worth remembering.

OVERLAY

Falling for you is spilling paint on carpet.
Sudden.
Unexpected.

I've tried my best, blotting out what had happened.
No matter how much I've managed to remove,
There will always be a soft spot
Invisible to the eye
But completely obvious to the heart.

QUIETUDE

There's something about silence in the morning.
You can hear life speak to you.
Whispers of truth ring in your ear.
Yells of anxiety and assertiveness
Echoing and intertwining.

We seldom notice how much skill comes into play
When drowning out the insignificant voices.
The darkness dimming our minds seem disheartening
Especially when the future is weighed out by stress.

Thoughts of losses are enough to keep you up at night.
But we must not put a figure on shortfalls
And build destruction out of thin air.
Remind yourself to count up all your happiness.

Sometimes, uncertainty is exciting.
Out of it, possibilities are born.
And where there is a possibility
There is life.

Death is certain yet unknown.
Though one thing is for sure,
Life outlives death every time.

LOST AND FOUND

Sometimes when we lose ourselves
we find out more about ourselves.
And every so often,
being out of your mind
is the best place to be.

CONTAINER

My smug eyes are bloodshot
from bottled up teardrops
spilling out of the blue
tipped over by devotion
slumped on the bitter floor
in the jet black basement
seeing red and feeling blue
refraining from speaking
my wobbling heart
will vocalize imperfections
it's unmanly to embody weakness
my ego aged 30 years
cracked open by life's unjust corkscrew
puncturing my bravado
silence is the answer
in unsettling times like these
but then you break it
by asking if I'm okay
my bumpy tone of voice
gives it away
I apologize for my transient frailty
you deflect it
because love always seems to understand.

CEMENTED REMINDER

It's easy to cave when caught in a dead zone.

If you're feeling stuck right now,
Remember,
Even a well-rooted tree still grows.

EVERYDAY THANKSGIVING

Thankful for
Being able
To be thankful.

GANDER

Take a look around you and really take it in.
See the sights,
Hear the sounds,
Smell the sin.
Feel the pain of single parents raising kids
Who turn to the streets
Because they can't see the light from within.

Take a glance at a very bright world.
Kids stuck in a trance,
Can't find the right turn.
Living on a fast lane
Where it's mad dark.
Blind by the cash game
And gained a black heart.

Somewhere along they picked up
The thought of never coming last place
Because Time's moving at a fast pace.
Now tell me how the earth is so plastic?
After all these years, things are still Jurassic.

The news seems old,
The world isn't getting younger.
Beauty covered by dirt,
The strong even suffer.
Remember
The sun comes after thunder.
And you don't have to starve to really feel the hunger.
Can't you see? Man, the struggle is real.
Innocent kids will literally kill for that one meal.

JIGSAW

We are all walking puzzles
Adjusting ourselves
To find our missing pieces.
When everything is said and done
In the fullness of time,
We all long to feel complete.

NOCTAMBULIST

We spend most of our lives sleepwalking.
It shouldn't take Death to appear
for us to open our eyes to Life.

MONEY or TIME

The landscaper is lining up the grass.
A posse of birds peck at the apples
on the slim tree.
The comfortable elderly sit in the shade
and watch them.
The flowers bloom freely.
The giddy tourists model
in front of the locally famous pillars.

Time is winging it
yet the ticker seems still.
The colour green surrounds me
a reminder of liberty and economy.
Freedom is pricy.
Time is a limited edition.

Some of us don't know freedom without funds.
What's the point of wealth without freedom?

Some days I wish for Time.
Sometimes I feel greedy for Money.
Is it just me?

While I'm balancing out which holds greater importance,
an engaged couple poses for the camera
without a care in the world.

The scale tips over.
Suddenly I realize what carries more weight.

SYMMETRY

I feel like I sneezed
unknowingly
in a certain way
and the universe "blessed me"
by interlacing our worlds.

Once we crossed paths,
I knew I wanted
to share my life with you
and desired to be
a part of yours.

It's almost as if it was
all written in the stars
that we were destined
to know each other in this lifetime
once more.

SCUFF

I'm walking on an empty road.
Strutting with a tormented soul.
Fighting emotions I can't control.
Heart pacing. . .
There's nowhere to go.

Why do we sometimes feel so alone?
Feeling out of place—
Even at home.

Eyes gazing at the stars,
Wondering how far I can go.
Within my heart, I feel a war.
Demons are trying to break guardian angels.

No time to be telling fables.
Everyone has cards on their tables.
Everybody falls,
It's about getting up from any rough angle.
Can you?

RIDGES

The devil is dancing on the clouds.
I'm standing on the corner of a cliff
getting an eyeful of the lake cycle towards the sand.
My friend clutching on a cold can of beer
gives voice to his love for his lady.
His heart is spouting through his teeth.
Devoted words are watering the dry grass.
The silent shrubs eavesdrop on our conversation.
He is gushing about his Diamond from Houston
and disclosing his yearning to wrap her in his arms.
I tune in on his joy,
smiling...
I can't help but be happy for him.

His faithfulness has me thinking of you.
I prayed we'd meet years before we met.
The angels continue to root for us.
I swear the Gods do as well.
It seems like we're worlds apart
but this invisible silver cord
binds us close.
At times I desperately wish
some scissors could cut
the distance that stands between us.
Racial barriers,
naysayers,
kilometres;
We surmount all the odds.
Love always finds its way.

NOTHING LASTS

I sent you an autumn bouquet
for your 28th birthday.
It made me think that
we unreservedly give
perishable things
to the people we love.

Our hearts wholly divided
fairly and unjustly distributed.
Our thoughts and efforts painfully fade
when Death seizes our existence.

I senselessly open the door
and there they are
sitting pretty on the graying wooden table.
Preserved, yet
still as colourful as they were two years ago.
My ageless love for you on display.

Some things last forever.

PULSE

This is a shout out to my family.
Even through insanity
We manage to live happily
Thanks for loving passively.

Through all these years
Blood, tears, and agony.
Damn, I can't believe
How blessed a man can be.

I'm grateful to have you here
By my side.
No goodbyes,
I'll see you next time.

And if I don't,
God forbid.
Just know
My love won't drift,
Even when I'm gone with the wind.

I can't tell you enough
How much it breaks my heart
For all the shame and pain I've caused in yours.

But I swear to God,
This guilt in my veins
Is the force
Pushing me towards
Making better changes.

Until I'm painless,

I want to make you proud.
Because it really does ache
To know I've let you down.
No more frowns
For now
Just smile for the moment.
Even if it's broken,
It's okay.
Keep hoping
For better days
Because hey,
Here they come.
I know things aren't always great
But we got to stay strong.
As the wind sails,
I'll never fail to love you more tomorrow,
No matter how long.

And I know it sounds weird,
Because I don't talk much.
I speak from right here,
Straight from the heart.

TRIED AND TRUE

People will call you arrogant and cocky
When you refuse to dilute
The truth of who you are.

People will disapprove
Because you choose not to conform
To their careless tailor-made idea of you.
How foolish it is
To let the opinions of others
Shape who you are.

Overstand yourself.
Hold your ground.
Why soften your strengths
To make those with weak characters
feel comfortable?

AWAKE

Raindrops crash on my window.
While the wind sings songs,
Lights flash like disco.
My pillows are covered in dreams
And anxiety.
What a surprise,
I can't fall asleep.

Another night counting sheep.
Oh, there goes sunlight…
What a creep.
Back on my feet
I can't seem to take a seat
On my ass—
Got my heart on my sleeve.

And I won't be relieved
Until my dreams are complete.
That's why my mind is always hungry to achieve.
Still
I humbly believe,
As long as I breathe,
I will succeed until I'm six-feet deep.

But even eternity couldn't stop me from living.
Not even a roadblock can halt this mission.
I'm so driven.

I KNOW HER

I know this lady who represents strength.
Real talk, 'cause she really doesn't pretend.
Independent woman,
She's as real as it gets.
She needs no man,
She isn't looking for a boyfriend.
Players can't comprehend
Trying to spit game.
Like, "God damn, girl. What's your name?"
"You got a lovely face, babe,"
"How's your day?".
She's grinning as if to say,
"Man, talk to the hand."

You'll never understand her ways.
That girl is Michael Jackson bad,
She knows how to act well behaved.
She'll slave just to eat like a queen.
Her heart is sweet -
Sure,
But she's still breaking men's dreams.

So many nights, she's up and can't sleep.
Unhappy with her life,
Feels stuck and digs deep.
But she's tough.
She fights through rough scenes.
And out of debris, she constructs what her heart speaks.

SOVEREIGNTY

Swallowing your pride
is the best remedy for your bruised ego.
We have to do what we must.
To move forward is the motive.

Sometimes those who have your heart the most
are the ones that have the least faith in you.
Never rely on other people to influence your self-belief.
Keep pressing ahead
even when no one has your back.

BROUGHT LOW

You are aware of everything around you
But not mindful of yourself.

To doubt who and what you are
Is to sign off an early grave
And ensure a life of mediocrity.

Tap out of slave mentality,
Tap into your mastery.
Who says you're not royalty
When you're the ruler of your world?

CATCH DRIFT

I can't allow myself to be driven by negative emotions.
They lead me to places I don't ever want to be in.
Somehow, I almost always find myself
Calling "shotgun,"
Jumping on the passenger seat,
And letting my emotions run through red lights.

I've done faced the airbag one too many times now.
Vision blurred by question marks,
My heart and mind scarred
By emotional shards.

Running wild
Without a destination.
I must take control
Before I'm led to calamity.

OBVIOUSLY

Anything fragile will shatter if it falls.
Never forget that your soul is made of steel.
The flesh can be easily broken.

You can always pick up what drops.
Most times, things that collapse rises to new heights.

Falling can be a blessing.
It cracks open the guard you've put up
concealing your greatest potential,
and then you discover what you're all about.

Falling can split the darkness
for you to catch a glimpse
of your inner light.

$U¢¢E$$

Success is a personal thing,
Not a selfish thing.
Success is growing.
Improving yourself every day,
Even if it's slightly.

Success is giving.
Giving your effort and dedication
To attain your goals.
Giving your love to those that are important to you.
Giving thanks for everything
That you are fortunate enough to have.
Even when you feel like you could have more.

Success is made up of fragments pieced together.
You make up your own design
Of how success will look like for you.
You don't need the same parts other people have.
All you need to have are
Upright values and principles.
That's what fashions true success.

FISHEYE

Those awkward seconds
when you're about to walk past a random person
who's heading in the opposite direction as you.
Most times, the mean mugs are priceless.

I don't blame those
who don't bother to make eye contact.
Since when is it a necessity
to have a staring contest with a stranger?
Supposedly the first one to look away is the loser.
Because apparently,
it's a sign of weakness.
See what the society has come to?

I find it funny when somebody makes a commotion
for the way someone else looks at them.
Those who claim to be "hard" start the drama.
But how tough are you really
if one glance can overpower you?

It's usually the ones who undermine people
that secretly feel others can destroy them.
And that's why they make a scene,
merely because they feel seen.

For those into staring contests with strangers,
it would be best if you faced yourself.
Take a good look at your existence.
That's the hardest shit there is.

SKIN DEEP

These so-called pretty girls
They're nearly all the same.
Brain full of pearls, shoes,
And diamond rings.
They say, every queen eventually finds her king.
In this world, in search of the finer things.

I see a pretty girl with her pretty lies.
Still,
She wonders why she always ends up with shitty guys.
Every night she feels like shit inside.
Sits and cries,
Bitches about life, wishing she died.

Questioning why
Does she feel so ugly.
Blind by city lights, sex, drugs and crushed dreams.
She speaks money,
That's what you call "buckteeth."
Stuck with a gritty mind
Thinking, "ONLY GOD CAN JUDGE ME."

Funny girl, she should know better.
Check herself before she sells her soul for cheddar.
I can't say it any clearer.
She's tasting her tears.
Her vision impaired by the face in the mirror.

2 of CUPS

we try to interpret this tarot card
zooming in on its mystery.
a red lion head floating
over two beings holding golden cups.

we state our guesswork
unconcerned with being wrong or right.

we're curious
to know the meaning.

but to me, I already knew
symbolically

these two were us.
enjoying the present

you being in mine
and me in yours.

sharing time
and returning smiles.

paying zero attention
to nothing else.

1+1
like divine mathematics,

unaltered,
unconditional.

CALL TO MIND

If you think
There's nothing to be thankful for,
Bear in mind
Your heart is beating at this very second.

Hear the mumble of each breath leaving your lungs.
Study the positives
Overbalancing all the bullshit that submerges
Your flooded brain.
Drain the pour of hatred that suffocates
Your divine nature.

Roll out the red carpet and usher in
Avalanches of love to sweep over your soul
Like a tsunami eating away dry land.

After all,
What's the greatest force in the world
That can smack some sense of gratitude into you?

FILTERED EXISTENCE

What pictures never show
Are the demons you've slain.
The heartbreaks you've had to stomach.
The blood, sweat and tears you've shed.
The restless nights.
The dreams you've manifested into reality.
The tormenting thoughts and voices you've drowned.
The guilt that has haunted you.
All of the mental barriers you've overcome.
All the fears you faced and laughed at.
All the poison that ate away at your heart.
All the deadweight that sat forcefully on your spirit.
All of the darkness you've shed light on.

Only you know how far you've come.
Only you know
What you've been through,
What you're going through,
Where you're going.
Don't let talk bother you.
Especially your own inner dialogue.
Rather than running your lip,
Be on your toes.
Don't be like most people
Who end up with their foot in their mouth.
Keep your feet on the ground,
But dream big.
Peace is power.
Don't give your power
Just because your peace disturbs
Those who are not in harmony with themselves.

Made in the USA
Monee, IL
09 February 2024